DATE DUE

15 MAY 12 '86	NOV 4 '86	SEP 30 '97
JAN 5 '87	SEP 23	
MAR 17 '87	MY 20 '97	
OCT 21 '87	OCT 23	
JAN 27 '88	APR 27	
MAY 15 '89		
MAY 31 '89	NO 3 00	
OCT 8 '90 12	JA 02 '01	
FEB 26 91 12	AP 5 01	
APR 24 91 11	FE 25 '02	
MAY 7 91	NO 20 02	
SEP 25 '92 11	SEP 19 03	
FEB 2 '95 7	SEP	
MAY 5 '95 5		
NOV 28 '95 15		
15		
FEB 5 '96 10		
MAY 21 96 29		
GAYLORD		PRINTED IN U.S.A.

BICYCLE MOTOCROSS
is for me

BICYCLE
MOTOCROSS
is for me

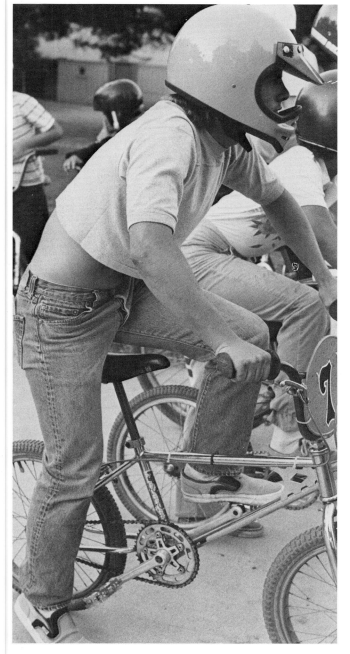

text **and photographs**
by Tom Moran

⅃ Lerner Publications Company   Minneapolis

This book was prepared under the supervision of Richard Lee and Ron Mackler, directors of the bicycle motocross program at Palms Recreation Center, Los Angeles, California. The author also wishes to thank Alex Siefert and those at the Cycle and Sport Shop, Santa Monica, California, and the World Wide BMX Program, San Fernando Valley Youth Foundation, Van Nuys, California, who helped with the book.

LIBRARY OF CONGRESS CATALOGING IN PUBLICATION DATA

Moran, Tom.
  Bicycle motocross is for me.

  (A Sports for me book)
  Summary: Describes the necessary equipment and the requirements for competition in bicycle motocross races.
    1. Bicycle motocross — Juvenile literature. [1. Bicycle motocross] I. Title II. Series: Sports for me books.
  GV1049.3.M67   796.6   81-20896
  ISBN 0-8225-1136-3   AACR2

Manufactured in the United States of America

International Standard Book Number: 0-8225-1136-3
Library of Congress Catalog Card Number: 81-20896

    3   4   5   6   7   8   9   10   91   90   89   88   87   86   85   84

Hi! My name is Kevin. My favorite sport is bicycle motocross, or BMX for short. BMX is a special kind of bike racing done on dirt courses. The competition is very exciting because the courses have jumps, sharp turns, and fast straight sections. I try to race as often as I can.

Most BMX racers use special bicycles
with 20-inch wheels. Younger riders whose
feet don't reach the pedals of regular bikes
can use smaller bicycles with 16-inch wheels.
These smaller bicycles are called **minis**.
Older racers sometimes use larger **cruiser**
bicycles with 26-inch wheels.

I have a regular BMX bicycle with 20-inch wheels. And I also have a **sidehack** racing bike. This is a three-wheeled cycle that carries two riders. The co-rider is called a **monkey.** He or she doesn't pedal but moves to help balance the bicycle.

All BMX bicycles are specially designed to handle the rough corners and jarring jumps of motocross competition. The owners of a bicycle shop near my home were very helpful in explaining the BMX parts to me.

The **frame** of your bike must be light and strong. The lighter it is, the less weight you have to pedal around the motocross course and the faster you can go. My racing bike weighs less than 25 pounds.

BMX bikes take a lot of punishment, so strength is important, too. Going off jumps, speeding over bumps, and colliding can bend and break bicycle frames if they are weak.

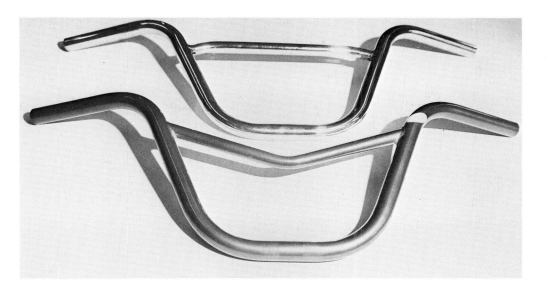

The **fork** is the part of the bicycle that holds the front wheel in place. The fork is connected to the handlebars by a **gooseneck.** Both must be very strong. A good bicycle shop will have a wide selection of these parts.

Your handlebars must be strong, too. Many kinds have a **crossbar** that helps to prevent them from bending. Special high-rise handlebars allow taller racers to steer the small BMX bicycles.

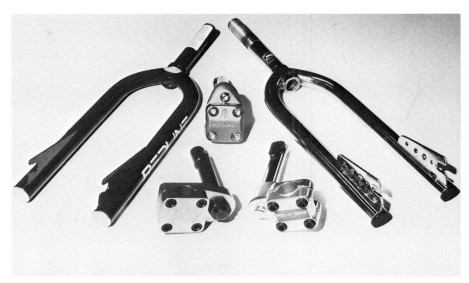

The wheels of a BMX bike must be strong enough to take the pounding and jarring of hard racing without bending. Some wheels are made of a rim and wire spokes. Many of these wheels have extra spokes for added strength. Other BMX wheels have large diameter spokes in many different styles. Wheels can be made from steel, aluminum, nylon, or other materials.

BMX tires must have good **tread** to be able to get a good grip on the race track surface. This gripping action is called **traction.** I use special **knobby** tires that are similar to the tires used by motorcycle racers. The rough tread gets good traction and gives me better control of my bike.

BMX races are held at motocross tracks all over the United States and in many other parts of the world, too. Some courses are very simple and can be set up on vacant land by adults. Many local and national motocross associations operate permanent tracks that can be very challenging.

Sharp turns, jumps, water hazards, and other trick sections make the races more exciting. Each track is different, and the racers must constantly think about the course in front of them.

I race at a park near my home. The course has both level and downhill runs between trees and bushes. Sometimes the track turns sharply around a tree, and I have to be careful not to bump into it. Sharp turns like this are called **hairpin turns**.

The races can get very rough. Racers often bump into each other at turns and tight corners. You can be disqualified for unnecessary bumping or crowding, but sometimes it can't be avoided. That's why good sportsmanship and fair play are so important.

The track rules where I race stress sportsmanship and safety. Before we are allowed to enter a race, our bicycles must be padded. We are also required to wear helmets. Our helmets are made of plastic and cushion the head when you fall. Some helmets are made with mouth guards to protect your teeth and face. Before I race, I always make sure that my helmet's chin strap is tied.

It can get very dusty in the middle of a crowded turn. So many riders use goggles, visors, and nose masks to protect them from flying pebbles and to help them see in the dust.

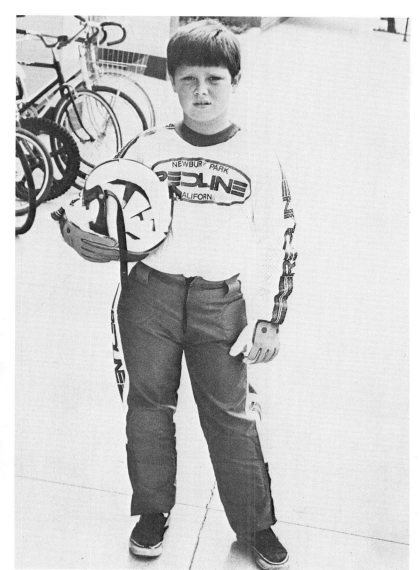

Some manufacturers make special padded shirts and pants for racers. But ordinary long-sleeved shirts and long pants can be worn, too. Most riders also wear gloves to protect their hands and to give them a better grip on the handlebars.

BMX bicycles are also equipped for safety. Rubber handgrips should be used to prevent the metal handlebar ends from cutting or hurting the riders. Plastic caps are available to cover the sharp ends of the bikes' axles. I use special snap-on pads for the most dangerous hard metal parts of my bike. You can make padding yourself using inexpensive foam and tape.

Sooner or later you are going to fall off your bicycle during a race. It happens to everybody. Racers call it **munching**. Sometimes it is called **crashing and burning** or **biting it**. Racers call falling over their handlebars an **endo.** The safety clothing and equipment help to prevent injuries during falls or crashes like these.

Although some crashes look very dangerous, no one should get seriously hurt if the racers are careful. When you munch or do an endo, try to roll away from your bicycle to cushion the fall. Do *not* roll away if there are other bike riders close behind you. At those times, tuck your arms and legs and stay very still so the other racers don't have to dodge a moving object.

I try not to get angry if I fall down or make a mistake during a race. The important thing is to try to improve. I try to learn what my mistakes are and not make them again. When I concentrate on improving, I have more fun, and my chances of doing well in the races are better, too.

I also learn a lot by watching and talking to the older racers at the track. They've given me lots of tips on how to handle my bike on turns and jumps.

I learned that the fastest path through a turn is called the **line.** It is usually the route from the outside edge of the track to the inside corner of the turn. Good racers pick the fastest line through every turn. But if someone has fallen on the turn or if a slower racer is in front of you, you can't always use the fastest line. You must quickly find a different route. If you are careful, turns can be a good place to pass other racers.

I also learned the best ways to race around different types of turns. Some turns are very wide, and you can go really fast through them. But you can slow down by braking before you get to the turn. My bicycle has **coaster brakes.** They are very simple to use. To stop or slow down, I only have to push backwards on the pedal. Then I can coast around the turn with my feet on the pedals.

The fastest way around hairpin turns is to slide around them. Many racers stick out their inside leg going into the turn. The stiff leg acts as a support and helps to maintain balance as you turn. Sometimes I use the bottom of my shoe to slightly slow the bike. But expert racers try to avoid doing this too much.

Some turns have dirt banks mounded along one side of them. These banked areas are called **berms**. To turn on a steep berm, you can go right along the side of the bank and pedal fast all the way through the turn.

The older racers also gave me some tips on handling **jumps**. Jumps are always included in every motocross event. They are very exciting. But because you lose time in the air, it's best to keep your bike low and hit the ground again as soon as possible.

Before going off a jump, pedal as fast as you can. When your bike is in the air, shift your weight backward and hold your front wheel up. Set your pedals to brace yourself and to cushion the impact of landing. That way you will be ready to start pedaling immediately when you land.

The landing is important. Land on the back wheel, and then shift your weight forward to bring the front wheel down. Take care not to land on your front wheel or on both wheels at the same time. If you land on your front wheel, you will do an endo. If you land on both wheels, there is a good chance that you will damage your bicycle.

Some racers turn their bicycles while they are in the air on a jump. This maneuver is called a **cross-up** and looks very spectacular to the crowd. But a cross-up does not help your racing position, and it's done mostly for show.

I try to avoid jumping too much or too far in a race. This saves me repair bills on my bicycle. I can't win races on a broken bike! But because bike parts do get bent or loosened, I always check my bicycle before each race to make sure it is in top shape.

I also make regular adjustments to my bike before each race. My friend often helps me. We always check the air pressure in the tires. The proper amount of air will depend on the track and its surface. When the track is soft, we put more air in the tires to make them roll easier. When the track is hard, we use less air for better traction.

We also change the **gears** for different track conditions. The gears are connected to the rear wheel and the pedal crank. The bicycle chain goes around them. The gears determine the number of times the rear wheel will turn for each complete turn of the pedal. I use gears that allow me to be at full speed on the longest straight section of the track.

I get to the track early on race days so that I can get my bike ready for competition. Then I find out what times my races begin. Motocross competition is made up of several short races called **motos.** Each racer runs several motos. You earn points for your place in the finish. You get one point for first place, two points for second place, and so on. The best riders are the ones with the lowest point scores in the motos. They go on to compete in a championship race called the **main event.**

Races are also divided into separate **classes** of riders. The classes are determined first by age group. Each age group is further divided into a **novice**, or amateur, class and an **expert** class. Beginning racers compete in novice classes. More experienced racers compete in expert classes. I race in the novice class for 11- and 12-year-old boys.

Girls race in special classes of their own. Girls' races are called **powder puff** races.

One of the most important parts of any moto is the start. From 3 to 12 bicycles will start at the same time, depending on how wide the track is.

Different tracks have different ways of starting races. Some use a **mechanical gate.** Others use an **elastic band** stretched across the starting line. The track where I race uses a **flagman** who signals the start with a flashlight.

You may start on either side of the bike, depending on which is more comfortable for you. I start with the bike on my right side. I tie my right pants leg so that it won't interfere with my pedaling. Some racers tuck their pants legs into their socks.

While I wait for the starting signal, I set my right pedal about one-third of the way from the top and rest my right foot on it. I keep my left foot on the ground to support myself. When the starter gives the signal, I put all my weight on the right pedal and push off with my left foot. I try to start pedaling as fast as I can to get the lead.

Concentration is very important at the start. I watch the starter very carefully and try to anticipate his signal. If you start too late, the other racers will get ahead of you. But if you start too soon, you may be disqualified or given penalty points.

Going around the race course is very exciting. You are going very fast, and you must make sharp turns and quick decisions. Everyone is bunched together and yelling for room. You have to be careful at all times and watch out for racers falling in front of you, obstacles on the track, and low-hanging tree branches.

Each moto is different. You never know who is going to win until you cross the finish line. For that reason, you must not give up if you fall down. I have fallen and have been the last to finish in a moto. Other times I have fallen and later caught up with all of the other racers. This is because they can make mistakes or fall, too.

Sometimes the flagman will change the course so that we have different obstacles and terrain to race over. We sometimes start at the end of the course and race toward the beginning.

Other times the flagman will vary the start of the motos. He might tell us to park our bikes upside down on the starting line. Then we race to them on foot and pick them up before we can start pedaling. Changes like these make each race interesting. It's like going to several different race courses.

One of the most exciting parts of the moto is the final stretch just before the finish line. On our course, you must pedal up a steep hill. It's very tiring. Then we turn down a long straight section of the track that ends at the finish line.

You can't slow down on the stretch or another racer can pass you easily. The spectators are all cheering and yelling encouragement to the riders. It's very exciting crossing the line, especially if you're first!

The final race of the season was very important to me. There were six riders in the main event, and we all knew each other. I got a very good start and was in second place coming into the first turn.

I stayed close to the leader through a series of hairpin turns and downhill over the rough terrain. We went off the final jump and into the last banked turn. I started to catch up to the lead racer. I pedaled as hard as I could. We were very close crossing the finish line.

When the flagman signaled and called my number, I was very happy. I had won the race! Afterward all of the racers shook my hand and congratulated me. We all knew we would be racing together again soon.

We had a ceremony after the race, and I was awarded a trophy. I'm going to put it in my room at home. I plan to keep racing, and I hope that I'll be in the junior expert class soon. Even if I don't win the next time I race, I know that I'll have fun. Bicycle motocross is for me!

Words about BMX RACING

BERM: A wall of dirt built up on the outside edge of a turn

BITE IT: A racer's term for a crash or collision

BMX: The abbreviation for bicycle motocross

COASTER BRAKE: A brake that works when the rider pedals in reverse

CRASH AND BURN: A racer's term for an especially hard fall or collision

CROSSBAR: A brace used to strengthen the handlebars on a racing bicycle

CROSS-UP: Turning the bike sideways in midair during a jump

CRUISER: A bicycle with large 26-inch wheels used in special BMX open classes

ELASTIC BAND: A method of starting BMX races using a stretched cord across the starting line

ENDO: A crash where the rider falls forward over the bike's handlebars

FLAGMAN: A BMX course official or race starter

FORK: The bicycle part that supports the front wheel

GEARS: Bicycle parts that are connected by the chain. The gears determine the number of times the rear wheel turns for each complete turn of the pedal.

GOOSENECK: The stem that connects the handlebars to the fork

HAIRPIN: An extremely tight turn on a race course

KNOBBIES: Special bicycle racing tires made for use in BMX

LINE: The fastest route around a race course turn

MAIN EVENT: The final race in BMX competition required when there are a large number of entries in a class

MECHANICAL GATE: A method of starting BMX races using a movable gate across the starting line

MINI: A small bicycle with 16-inch wheels used by younger riders in BMX

MONKEY: The passenger in a sidehack

MOTO: A preliminary race in BMX competition

MUNCH: A racer's term for a fall or crash

POWDER PUFF: A special BMX class for girl racers

SIDEHACK: A three-wheeled cycle that carries two riders

TRACTION: The ability to get a good bite or hold on the race track surface

ABOUT THE AUTHOR/PHOTOGRAPHER

TOM MORAN is a freelance writer and the author of two photographic books and several books in the *Sports For Me* series. He has coached youth football, soccer, and boxing, and he frequently writes on sports subjects for California magazines and newspapers. Mr. Moran lives in Venice, California.